D1289055

Published in 2014 by The Rosen Publishing Group, Inc.
29 East 21st Street, New York, NY 10010

Copyright © 2014 Weldon Owen Pty Ltd. Originally published in 2011 by Discovery Communications, LLC.

Original copyright © 2011 Discovery Communications, LLC. Discovery Education™ and the Discovery Education logo are trademarks of Discovery Communications, LLC, used under license. All rights reserved.

All rights reserved. No part of this book may be reproduced in any form without permission in writing from the publisher, except by a reviewer.

Photo Credits: **KEY** tl=top left; tc=top center; tr=top right; c=center; cr=center right; bl=bottom left; bc=bottom center; br=bottom right

CBT = Corbis; iS = istockphoto.com; N = NASA; SH = Shutterstock; TF = Topfoto

Cover, **28**tr CBT; **10–11**tc N; **15**br CBT; **18–19**bc iS; **26**bl CBT; c TF; tl SH; **29**bl CBT; c, cr, tr N; tl SH

All illustrations copyright Weldon Owen Pty Ltd

Weldon Owen Pty Ltd
Managing Director: Kay Scarlett
Creative Director: Sue Burk
Publisher: Helen Bateman
Senior Vice President, International Sales: Stuart Laurence
Vice President Sales North America: Ellen Towell
Administration Manager, International Sales: Kristine Ravn

Publisher's Cataloging Data

Coupe, Robert.
Volcanoes: fire from below / by Robert Coupe.
p. cm. — (Discovery education: earth and space science)
Includes index..
ISBN 978-1-4777-6186-1 (library binding) — ISBN 978-1-4777-6188-5 (pbk.) — ISBN 978-1-4777-6189-2 (6-pack)
1. Volcanoes — Juvenile literature. I. Coupe, Robert. II. Title.
QE521.3 C68 2014
363.34—d23

Manufactured in the United States of America

CPSIA Compliance Information: Batch #W14PK2: For Further Information contact Rosen Publishing, New York, New York at 1-800-237-9932

EARTH AND SPACE SCIENCE

VOLCANOES
FIRE FROM BELOW

ROBERT COUPE

New York

Contents

Restless Planet

The ground we walk on and the homes that we live in may seem to be still, but they are not. That is because our planet, Earth, is never at rest. It is spinning in space as it moves in orbit around the Sun. The top part of Earth's surface is also slowly shifting, and not far below the crust, there is a constant movement of molten magma within the mantle.

Hot, rocky layers

Below Earth's crust there are other layers of rock. First comes the mantle, where the rock is so hot it can flow, and even melt to form magma that sometimes forces its way to the surface. Beneath the mantle lies the hot, liquid outer core. At the very center, the core becomes solid because of the tremendous weight of all the rock above it.

Earth through the ages

The planet Earth was formed 4.6 billion years ago, when dust and gas that circled the Sun were pulled together by the force of gravity. For most of the time that Earth has existed, the only life forms were simple bacteria. More complex life forms began to appear about 550 million years ago.

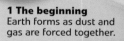

1 The beginning
Earth forms as dust and gas are forced together.

2 Collision
A small, infant planet crashes into Earth.

3 The Moon
Rocks fly into space and form the Moon.

4 Cooling down
As Earth cools down, land and oceans form.

Crust

Outer mantle

Lower mantle

Outer core

Inner core

EARTH'S CRUST

The crust of Earth is made up mainly of two types of rock: granite and basalt. These are both igneous rocks that formed from magma after it cooled. The crust is much thinner under the oceans than it is under the great landmasses of Earth, which are the continents.

Underwater
Here the crust can be as thin as 3 miles (5 km) deep.

Under land
Here, the crust can be up to 45 miles (70 km) deep.

Collision Course

The Earth's crust is made of vast, rocky slabs called tectonic plates that are always moving. When the plates hit each other, they can cause earthquakes, or they can be pushed upward to form mountains. If magma from the mantle comes up through these mountains, they can erupt as volcanoes.

The Himalayas
These vast and mighty mountains, in the north of India, formed slowly as huge tectonic plates crashed together.

1 Plates moving
About 200 million years ago, the land that is now India began to move northward toward Asia.

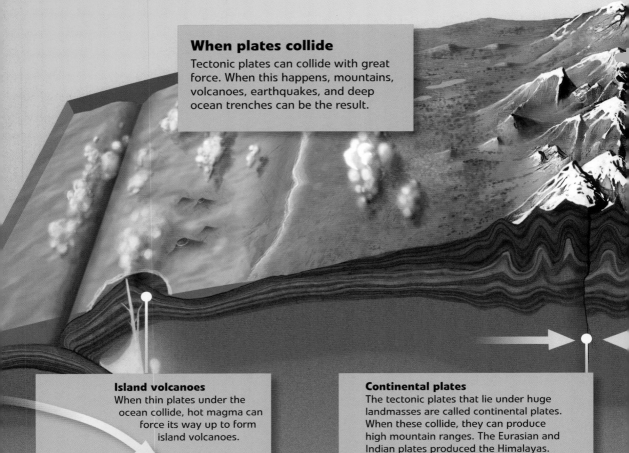

When plates collide
Tectonic plates can collide with great force. When this happens, mountains, volcanoes, earthquakes, and deep ocean trenches can be the result.

Island volcanoes
When thin plates under the ocean collide, hot magma can force its way up to form island volcanoes.

Continental plates
The tectonic plates that lie under huge landmasses are called continental plates. When these collide, they can produce high mountain ranges. The Eurasian and Indian plates produced the Himalayas.

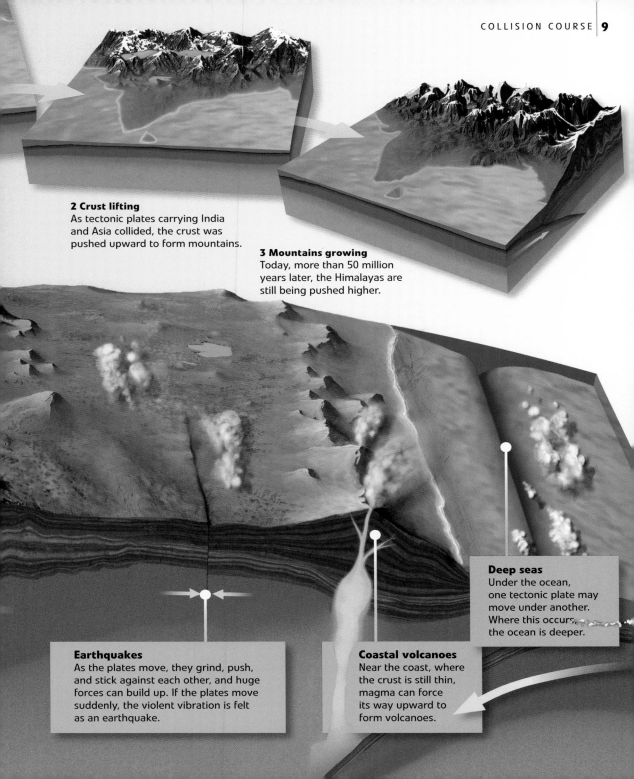

2 Crust lifting
As tectonic plates carrying India and Asia collided, the crust was pushed upward to form mountains.

3 Mountains growing
Today, more than 50 million years later, the Himalayas are still being pushed higher.

Deep seas
Under the ocean, one tectonic plate may move under another. Where this occurs, the ocean is deeper.

Earthquakes
As the plates move, they grind, push, and stick against each other, and huge forces can build up. If the plates move suddenly, the violent vibration is felt as an earthquake.

Coastal volcanoes
Near the coast, where the crust is still thin, magma can force its way upward to form volcanoes.

Hot Spots

I n some parts of the world, hot magma forces itself violently up through Earth's crust. The places where this happens are called hot spots. Because a tectonic plate moves very slowly over a hot spot, a volcano can form above the hot spot. Then, as millions of years pass and the plate keeps moving farther on while the hot spot stays in the same place, a line of volcanoes can form over the same hot spot.

Oceanic hot spot

Some hot spots beneath the ocean create volcanoes. These form and then slowly die away over many millions of years as the moving plate carries them away. At first, the erupting magma forms an underwater volcano. The mountain grows until it emerges above the ocean surface as a volcanic island.

Volcano
A volcano forms over the hot spot.

Hot spot
Magma forces its way up through Earth's crust.

Earth's tectonic plates are moving at a speed of up to 4 inches (10 cm) every year.

Hot spot Hawaii

This photo of hot spot islands in Hawaii was taken from space. The largest island, which is known as the Big Island, is directly over a hot spot beneath the ocean. It is a combination of five separate volcanos. When each of the other islands was over the hot spot, each one of them was a volcano, too. Now these islands are slowly sinking back into the sea.

Shrinking
The former volcano shrinks to become a small island.

Moving away
The former volcano gets smaller as it moves away from the hot spot.

Tectonic plate
The plate continues to move very slowly.

That's Amazing!

When hot spots occur below the ocean, volcanoes grow up very slowly from the seafloor. It takes these volcanoes about 1 million years to reach the ocean surface.

Crater
Inside the top of the
volcano, the crater is usually
the major source of lava and
gases in an eruption.

Side vent
Magma flows out
through a vent
in the side of
the volcano.

Fact or Fiction?

A myth from Hawaii tells of Pele,
goddess of fire and volcanoes. She
lives inside the volcano Kilauea, and
when she is angry, she hurls fire into
the air and hot lava across the land.

Laccolith
Some magma flows
into a chamber called a
laccolith. It cools down
and does not flow
to the surface.

A Volcano Erupts

Magma is very hot, thick, liquid rock. It forms when great heat causes rock in Earth's mantle to melt. This melted rock then forms into large underground chambers. In places, the magma forces its way upward through cracks in Earth's crust to form a volcano. A buildup of pressure causes the volcano to erupt. Steam, ash, and fragments of rock rise high in the air and hot lava flows down the mountainside.

Cone
The cone is the outside of the volcano. It is built up from lava and ash from earlier eruptions.

Central conduit
This is the main channel that leads from the chamber of magma to the crater.

Dike
When magma cuts up through the layers of surrounding rock, it is called a dike and may emerge through the surface as a vent.

Channels and vents

The inside of a volcano is made of solid rock. Inside this rock are chambers or channels of hot magma. At times, magma forces its way through a side channel and comes out through a vent in the side of the volcano.

Fissure
Magma can erupt through a long line of vents. They are called fissure eruptions.

Pyroclastic flow
A fluid mixture of lava fragments and toxic gas races down the volcano.

Fireworks
As it erupts, a volcano can create a fountain of lava above its crater.

Different eruptions

No two volcano eruptions are exactly the same. All the things in this picture happen when volcanoes erupt, but they would be very unlikely to all occur together during one single eruption.

Coils
As lava flows, it spreads out to cover the ground. Some lava spreads in folds that look like coils of rope. It is called pahoehoe lava.

Lava and Ash

That's Amazing!
In April 2010, a volcano in Iceland erupted. Its spreading ash made it dangerous for aircraft to fly, so, for several days, there were no flights into or out of European airports.

When a volcano erupts, hot rock and ash explode high into the air. The rock then drops back and down the sides of the volcano. It can bring death and destruction to living things in its way. The ash spurts far above the volcano and often forms thick, dirty clouds.

Lava tube breakout
Lava can flow a long way through channels just beneath the surface before breaking out far from the crater.

Fissure
Lava erupts through a series of side vents, called fissures, and creates a curtain of fire.

Molten lava
As hot lava snakes down the mountainside, it sets fire to buildings and trees in its path.

Overview
A view from the air shows lava erupting from the crater of the Kilauea volcano, in Hawaii, and flowing away.

Falling rock
Chunks of melted rock cool and turn solid as they hurtle through the air, then crash downward.

Studying Volcanoes

People who study volcanoes are called volcanologists. They are scientists who use aircraft and spacecraft to record when and where volcanoes erupt and the effects of these eruptions. But volcanologists also climb into the craters of volcanoes, where they collect samples of lava and take measurements. These help them work out how the volcano is behaving now and what it has done in the past.

Gas detector
This machine measures gases that come out when a volcano erupts.

VOLCANOLOGIST

To become a volcanologist, you will need:

INTERESTS: Enjoy working outdoors and be adventurous. Be curious and like solving puzzles.

EDUCATION: Study mathematics, geography, and science subjects in high school. Complete a science degree at college, with a major in geology. Gain a postgraduate degree in geology or volcanology.

Helmet

Special protective clothing

Keeping safe
A special thermal suit protects a volcanologist from the heat.

Instrument for gathering lava samples

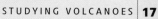

Getting in
Helicopters allow volcanologists to get to volcanoes in remote places and to land near them. These helicopter flights can be extremely dangerous.

TOP 10 ON-SITE HAZARDS

1 Intense heat

2 Poisonous gases

3 Falling rocks

4 Hot ash

5 Acid rain

6 Windstorms

7 Unstable ground

8 Sudden or hidden lava flow

9 Altitude sickness

10 Poor visibility

Collecting lava samples
To collect samples of lava, a volcanologist needs to get very close to lava as it flows down a mountainside soon after a volcanic eruption. When close to hot lava, volcanologists often work, for safety, in teams of two or more.

All About Volcanoes

Different volcanoes
There are different kinds of volcanoes. They are formed from different types of rock, have different shapes, and erupt in different ways.

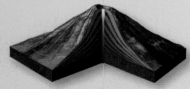

Cinder cone
Eruptions build up cone-shaped hills of cinders with wide craters.

Composite or stratovolcano
When these erupt, they build up layers of ash and lava.

Shield
These broad, low volcanoes are formed entirely from lava.

Fissure
These volcanoes form when magma erupts through a crack in Earth's surface.

MEASURING ERUPTIONS
The amount of material that erupts from a volcano, known as the eruptive volume, gives a good idea of how powerful that volcano is. The amount, measured in cubic miles or cubic kilometers, varies greatly, from small house-size deposits to huge eruptions that can be millions of times bigger.

Toba
670 mi³
(2,800 km³)

Taupo
25 mi³
(100 km³)

ARCTIC
OCEAN

EUROPE

ASIA

AFRICA

ATLANTIC
OCEAN

INDIAN
OCEAN

AUSTRALIA

ANTARCTICA

Danger zones
Most volcanic eruptions happen along the edges of tectonic plates or over hot spots. The most dangerous are near where many people live, such as in Indonesia.

Elevation (ft.)

20,000
15,000
10,000
5,000
Sea level
−5,000
−10,000
−15,000
−20,000

Elevation (m)

6,000
4,000
2,000
Sea level
−2,000
−4,000
−6,000

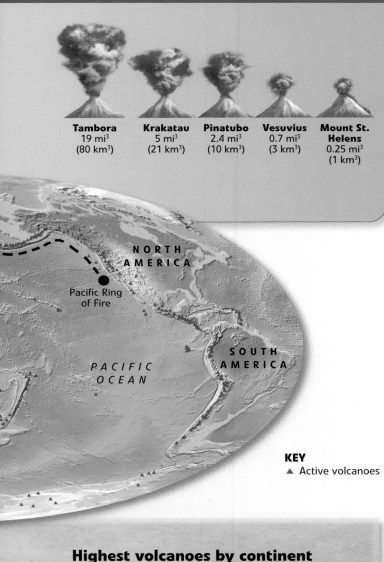

Tambora | **Krakatau** | **Pinatubo** | **Vesuvius** | **Mount St. Helens**
19 mi³ | 5 mi³ | 2.4 mi³ | 0.7 mi³ | 0.25 mi³
(80 km³) | (21 km³) | (10 km³) | (3 km³) | (1 km³)

NORTH AMERICA

Pacific Ring of Fire

PACIFIC OCEAN

SOUTH AMERICA

KEY
▲ Active volcanoes

Highest volcanoes by continent

Although many mountains have higher summits, Hawaii's Mauna Kea is the greatest mountain on Earth. If you measure it from its base on the ocean floor, Mauna Kea towers at more than 31,000 feet (9,500 m).

1 Nevado Ojos del Salado, South America

2 Kilimanjaro, Africa

3 Damavand, Asia

4 Elbrus, Europe

5 Pico de Orizaba, North America

6 Mount Sidley, Antarctica

7 Mauna Kea, Hawaii

Types of eruptions

Scientists who study volcanoes use the following names to describe different kinds of eruptions.

Hawaiian
Fountains and rivers of lava erupt from the crater, vents, and fissures. The lava flows create wide, low shield volcanoes.

Strombolian
Falling rock, ash, and cinders build tall cones, which may collapse if the sides of the cone become too steep.

Vulcanian
Violent explosions blast large rocks and lava bombs high into the air. These can often spread over a wide area.

Plinian
These large explosions empty the volcano's magma chambers and produce huge ash clouds that can rise 30 miles (48 km) high. Ultra-Plinian explosions are even more powerful.

Peléean
A dome of hard lava in the crater collapses, producing fast-moving flows of hot gas, rock, and ash.

Famous Volcanoes

Toba
Eruptive volume:
670 mi³
(2,800 km³).

La Garita
Eruptive volume:
1,200 mi³
(5,000 km³)

BIGGER BANG

Toba's eruption was huge, but we know of one that was almost twice as big. It happened 27 million years ago in the US, long before any humans existed.

Particular volcanoes become famous when they erupt and cause enormous amounts of damage. Perhaps the most famous of all is Mount Vesuvius in southern Italy. Almost 2,000 years ago, it suddenly erupted and destroyed two nearby towns.

Awesome ash cloud
After Toba erupted, a cloud of ash spread around the world. In areas near Toba, it formed a layer 30 feet (9 m) thick on the ground.

Toba

About 73,500 years ago, this volcano, on the island of Sumatra, in Indonesia, erupted and sent ash and gases all around the world. This caused Earth to cool down dramatically for six years.

TOBA: THE FACTS

When it erupted: About 73,500 years ago

Type of eruption: Ultra-Plinian

Eruptive volume: About 670 cubic miles (2,800 km³)

People killed: Not known

Spreading haze
The layer of ash and gases that surrounded Earth after the eruption partly blocked out the Sun's rays. As a result, there was a very long winter everywhere in the world.

Altitude	
mi	km
15	25
	20
10	15
5	10
	5
0	0

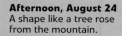

Afternoon, August 24
A shape like a tree rose from the mountain.

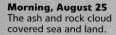

Evening, August 24
Ash and rocks fell onto ships at sea.

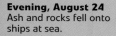

Morning, August 25
The ash and rock cloud covered sea and land.

Vesuvius

In August AD 79, Mount Vesuvius erupted, covering the cities of Pompeii and Herculaneum with hot ash, rock, and poisonous gases. Some people managed to escape but many died.

VESUVIUS: THE FACTS

When it erupted: August AD 79

Type of eruption: Combination of Plinian and Vulcanian

Eruptive volume: About 0.7 cubic miles (3 km³)

People killed: Between 3,000 and 10,000

1 Hot ash
A person dies, covered with hot ash.

2 Discovered
After the skeleton is discovered, it is covered with plaster.

Making models
Modern scientists were able to make models of some of the people who died when Vesuvius erupted.

3 Preserved
The plaster sets and leaves a perfect cast of the body.

Krakatau

The series of eruptions on August 27, 1883, destroyed the island of Krakatau. Gas and ash blocked out the sunlight and brought cooler weather to nearby areas. A new volcano, Anak Krakatau, has since begun to grow up from the seafloor where Krakatau once stood.

KRAKATAU: THE FACTS

When it erupted: August 27, 1883

Type of eruption: Combination of Plinian and ultra-Plinian

Eruptive volume: 5 cubic miles (21 km³)

People killed: 36,417

The sounds of Krakatau's eruptions were so loud they could be heard 2,800 miles (4,500 km) away.

Destruction

The enormous amounts of hot ash and rock that poured into the sea after the eruption caused huge tidal waves. These spread to nearby islands and to other parts of Indonesia, destroying towns and villages and killing many people and animals.

The Daily News

KRAKATAU ERUPTS!

Violent Explosions Kill 36,000

A series of powerful eruptions has occurred on the volcanic island of Krakatau in the Dutch East Indies, north of Australia. Reports indicate that these are some of the largest volcanic eruptions ever witnessed.

More than 36,000 people in the area are believed to have died as huge tidal waves spread through the region, swamping settlements on other islands and destroying towns and villages.

Huge explosions

Krakatau was a volcanic island in the Indonesian archipelago. In mid-1883, its volcano began to erupt. The eruptions grew bigger until, on August 27, there were four huge explosions over a period of about four hours. The last eruption was the largest and loudest of them all, and it was the most powerful volcanic eruption that people had ever seen. It sent clouds of gas and ash 50 miles (80 km) up into the air.

No surprise

This eruption was not a surprise, but perhaps the size of it was. For months, scientists had been watching the growing bulge on the mountain's side. They knew that a blast would not be long in coming.

1

March–May 1980
Magma builds up in a chamber inside the volcano. The side of the mountain begins to bulge outward.

2

08:32:37, May 18
Early in the morning, the side of the mountain gives way. There is a huge landslide and blast at both the top and side of the mountain.

Mount St. Helens

In March 1980, in Washington State, this volcano had a small eruption. Then a bulge appeared on the mountain. It kept growing bigger. On May 18, one whole side of the mountain blew out.

MOUNT ST. HELENS: THE FACTS

When it erupted: May 18, 1980

Type of eruption: Plinian

Eruptive volume: 0.25 cubic miles (1 km³)

People killed: 57

That's Amazing!

The Mount St. Helens blast sent ash over much of the Pacific Northwest. Some ash traveled east as far as Oklahoma. That is almost halfway across the country.

Flattened forest
The volcanic blast destroyed vast areas of forest as ash and lava flowed through them.

Lahar flow
Just after the eruption, a hot flow of hot ash and water, known as a lahar, rushed down from the mountain.

Falling ash
Ash from the volcano rained down on towns in the Pacific Northwest in the days afterward.

3

08:32:41, May 18
Moments later, the crater blasts wide open. A huge mass of ash, rock, and gas is thrown up. It reaches 12 miles (19 km) into the atmosphere.

Spreading lava
The constant flow of lava from Kilauea since 1983 has now covered about 40 square miles (10,400 ha). It has increased the actual area of Big Island by about 0.5 square miles (121 ha).

Destruction
So far, lava from Kilauea has destroyed at least 189 homes. It has also ruined areas of national parkland and damaged roads.

Kilauea

Kilauea is on the southeast corner of the Big Island of Hawaii. It lies over a hot spot in the Pacific Ocean. It erupts gently but constantly, and produces spectacular fountains of fire and long flows of lava. Thousands of people visit to get a very close view of Kilauea.

KILAUEA: THE FACTS

When it erupted: Has been erupting almost constantly since 1983

Type of eruption: Hawaiian

Eruptive volume: 0.7 cubic miles (2.9 km³)

People killed: Some careless visitors have died from falling or by breathing in toxic gases

Volcanoes that bring death

Over the centuries, volcanoes around the world have killed huge numbers of people. Most deaths are caused by the hot ash and poisonous gases. Some people are killed by the huge ocean waves, or tsunamis, that an eruption can create.

Volcano	Year	Number of deaths
1 Tambora Indonesia	1815	92,000
2 Krakatau Indonesia	1883	36,417
3 Mount Pelée Martinique	1902	29,025
4 Nevado del Ruiz Colombia	1985	25,000
5 Mount Unzen Japan	1792	14,300
6 Laki Iceland	1783	9,350
7 Kelut Indonesia	1882	5,110
8 Galunggung Indonesia	1882	4,011
9 Mount Vesuvius Italy	1631	3,500
10 Mount Vesuvius Italy	AD 79	3,000–10,000

Black beaches
Volcanic islands have black beaches, like this one on Maui, Hawaii. The sand of these beaches is made from basalt. This is an igneous rock that forms when lava cools. It then breaks down into sand particles.

Fast flow
Hot lava can move as fast as 60 miles (100 km) per hour. It slows down as it cools. Eventually, it becomes solid.

Active, dormant, and extinct
There are about 1,500 active volcanoes around the world, but there are many more that are dormant or extinct. Here are some notable examples.

KEY
= Active volcano
= Dormant volcano
= Extinct volcano
= Last eruption

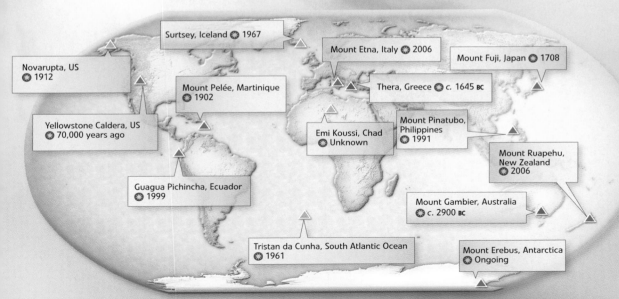

Surtsey, Iceland 🌣 1967

Novarupta, US 🌣 1912

Mount Etna, Italy 🌣 2006

Mount Fuji, Japan 🌣 1708

Mount Pelée, Martinique 🌣 1902

Thera, Greece 🌣 c. 1645 BC

Yellowstone Caldera, US 🌣 70,000 years ago

Mount Pinatubo, Philippines 🌣 1991

Emi Koussi, Chad 🌣 Unknown

Mount Ruapehu, New Zealand 🌣 2006

Guagua Pichincha, Ecuador 🌣 1999

Mount Gambier, Australia 🌣 c. 2900 BC

Tristan da Cunha, South Atlantic Ocean 🌣 1961

Mount Erebus, Antarctica 🌣 Ongoing

Diamonds
The extreme heat and pressure in Earth's mantle can create diamonds. Rising magma then pushes these diamonds to the surface of Earth.

Volcano Facts

Volcanoes have brought fascination and fear to humans for thousands of years, and their secrets continue to be revealed by volcanologists. Here are some more facts and figures about volcanoes, both on Earth and in other parts of our solar system.

Vulcan
The word volcano comes from Vulcan, the Roman god of fire. The ancient Romans believed that he caused volcanoes to erupt.

VOLCANOES OUT OF THIS WORLD

Volcanoes do not occur only on Earth. They are also on a number of other planets and on some of the moons in our solar system.

The Moon
Dark patches on the Moon are lakes of solid lava. Billions of years ago, this lava erupted from fissures in the surface.

Mars
Mars is only about half as big as Earth, but it has volcanoes that make even our tallest volcanoes seem tiny by comparison. They are now almost certainly extinct.

Venus
Venus has thousands of volcanoes. That is why it has such a thick atmosphere. Some of these may still be active, but scientists do not know for certain yet.

Triton
Volcanoes are not always hot. In 1989, a passing space probe discovered enormous geysers on Neptune's largest moon, Triton, that erupt with supercold liquid nitrogen.

Io
There is more volcanic activity on Jupiter's moon Io than anywhere else in the solar system. Large amounts of sulfur dioxide, both in gas and liquid form, spew from its surface.

Test Your Knowledge

In the left column below are some descriptions. In the right column are scrambled words. Can you unscramble the letters of the words in the right column and then match up each word with its description?

A

1 The part of Earth above the mantle

2 Melted rock below Earth's surface

3 The top part of a volcano

4 Hot liquid that erupts from a volcano

5 How we describe a volcano that still erupts

6 What a volcano does

7 A planet in our Solar System that has many volcanoes on it

8 An ancient volcano in Indonesia

B

NUEVS

EACTVI

RUPEST

REACTR

BOAT

GAAMM

VAAL

RSCTU

Answers: 1 CRUST 2 MAGMA 3 CRATER 4 LAVA 5 ACTIVE 6 ERUPTS 7 VENUS 8 TOBA

Glossary

acid rain (A-sud RAYN)
Rain, sleet, or snow that contains chemicals that are harmful to people, animals, and plants.

active volcano
(AK-tiv vol-KAY-noh)
A volcano that erupts regularly or from time to time. Eruptions from an active volcano can be years, or even centuries, apart.

ash (ASH)
Sand or dust-sized pieces of rock that fly out of a volcano when it is erupting.

bacteria (bak-TEER-ee-uh)
Tiny living things, each consisting of only one cell.

core (KOR)
The very center of Earth. It consists of a solid inner core, and a molten outer core.

crust (KRUST)
The solid, outer part of Earth. It is the top layer of our planet. It is about 25 miles (40 km) deep. We live on Earth's crust but the bottom of the oceans is also part of Earth's crust.

dormant volcano
(DOR-munt vol-KAY-noh)
A volcano that has not erupted for a long time but that could erupt again.

extinct volcano
(ik-STINGKT vol-KAY-noh)
A volcano that has not erupted for a very long time and that will probably never erupt again.

fissure (FIH-shur)
A large crack, or fracture, in the ground. A line of vents can cause a fissure in a volcano.

hot spot (HOT SPOT)
A place where magma is constantly coming up through Earth's crust.

igneous rock
(IG-nee-us ROK)
Rock that is formed when magma cools down and turns solid.

laccolith (LA-ku-lith)
A chamber inside a volcano into which magma flows and then cools down. This magma may push rocks above it upward.

lahar (LAH-har)
Hot mud that flows down the sides of a volcano after it has erupted.

lava (LAH-vuh)
Melted rock that flows out of a volcano during an eruption. Hot lava can travel for long distances over the ground.

magma (MAG-muh)
Melted rock that is inside Earth, below the crust.

mantle (MAN-tul)
The thick, hot layer inside Earth between the crust and the core. Magma forms inside the mantle.

pahoehoe
(puh-HOH-ee-hoh-ee)
A type of lava flow that is smooth and that forms coils like rope.

pyroclastic flow
(py-roh-KLAS-tik FLOH)
A thick, heated mixture of gas, ash, and fragments of rock that flows at great speed down the sides of a volcano.

tectonic plates
(tek-TAH-nik PLAYTZ)
Vast sheets of rock that move constantly beneath Earth's surface. All of Earth's surface sits on tectonic plates.

tidal wave (TY-dul WAYV)
A huge ocean wave that can cause great destruction when it hits a coastline. Tidal waves are usually caused by earthquakes under the sea.

vent (VENT)
An opening at the top or side of a volcano through which lava, gas, and ash flow out.

Index

Websites

Due to the changing nature of Internet links, PowerKids Press has developed an online list of websites related to the subject of this book. This site is updated regularly. Please use this link to access the list:

www.powerkidslinks.com/disc/volcan/